IT
SHIT
ENS HAPPENS SHIT HA
SO
GET
T OVER IT OVER IT OVE

D0854356

SHIT SHIT SHIT
PPENS HAPPENS HAPPENS
SO SO SO
ET GET GET
R IT OVER IT OVER IT

IT SHIT SHIT
ENS HAPPENS HAPPENS HA
SO SO
GET GET G
T OVER IT OVER IT OVE

SHIT SHIT SHIT
PPENS HAPPENS HAPPENS
SO SO SO
ET GET GET
R IT OVER IT OVER IT

SHIT HAPPENS SO GET OVER IT

SHIT
HAPPENS
SO
GET
OVER IT

summersdale

SHIT HAPPENS SO GET OVER IT

Summersdale Publishers Ltd
46 West Street
Chichester
West Sussex
PO19 1RP
UK

www.summersdale.com

Printed and bound in the Czech Republic

ISBN: 978-1-84953-132-0

Substantial discounts on bulk quantities of Summersdale books are available to corporations, professional associations and other organisations. For details contact Summersdale Publishers by telephone: +44 (0) 1243 771107, fax: +44 (0) 1243 786300 or email: nicky@summersdale.com.

SHIT
HAPPENS
SO
GET
OVER IT

If you are going
through hell, keep
going.

Winston Churchill

To succeed in life, you need three things: a wishbone, a backbone and a funny bone.

Reba McEntire

Let life happen to you.
Believe me, life is in
the right, always.

Rainer Maria Rilke

Nobody can go back and start a new beginning, but anyone can start today and make a new ending.

Maria Robinson

What's done is done.

William Shakespeare, *Macbeth*

Genius is divine
perseverance.

Woodrow T. Wilson

If you can find a path
with no obstacles, it
probably doesn't
lead anywhere.

Frank A. Clark

Don't go around saying the world owes you a living. The world owes you nothing. It was here first.

Mark Twain

Sometimes you just
have to pee in
the sink.

Charles Bukowski

You may not realise it when
it happens, but a kick in the
teeth may be the best thing
in the world for you.

Walt Disney

Life doesn't imitate
art, it imitates bad
television.

Woody Allen

Some days you're the bug.
Some days you're
the windshield.

Price Cobb

You can't be brave if you've
only had wonderful things
happen to you.

Mary Tyler Moore

Life: it is about the gift, not the package it comes in.

Dennis P. Costea Jr

If we had no winter, the spring would not be so pleasant; if we did not sometimes taste of adversity, prosperity would not be so welcome.

Anne Bradstreet

Sometimes you can
get a splinter even
sliding down
a rainbow.

Cherralea Morgen

Never complain and never explain.

Benjamin Disraeli

Stand up and walk out of
your history.

Phil McGraw

If you only do what you
know you can do – you
never do very much.

Tom Krause

Anyone who trades
liberty for security
deserves neither.

Benjamin Franklin

Accept the impossible, do
without the indispensable,
and bear the intolerable.

Kathleen Norris

Do not spoil what you have by desiring what you have not.

Epicurus

People have to really
suffer before they can
risk doing what
they love.

Chuck Palahniuk

Perseverance is failing
nineteen times and
succeeding the twentieth.

Julie Andrews

Live today for
tomorrow it will all
be history.

Proverb

There are days when it takes all you've got just to keep up with the losers.

Robert Orben

Life only demands from you
the strength you possess.
Only one feat is possible –
not to run away.

Dag Hammarskjöld

When your dreams turn to dust, vacuum.

Desmond Tutu

Experience is what you get
when you don't get what
you want.

Dan Stanford

Life is simple, it's just not easy.

Anonymous

Learn from yesterday, live for today, hope for tomorrow. The important thing is not to stop questioning.

Albert Einstein

Do what you can,
with what you have,
where you are.

Theodore Roosevelt

Life is just one damned thing after another.

Elbert Hubbard

In three words I can sum
up everything I've learned
about life: it goes on.

Robert Frost

Life isn't about waiting
for the storm to pass;
it's about learning to
dance in the rain.

Anonymous

I have sometimes been wildly, despairingly, acutely miserable… but through it all I still know… to be alive is a grand thing.

Agatha Christie

When I hear somebody sigh, 'Life is hard,' I am always tempted to ask, 'Compared to what?'

Sydney J. Harris

Without some goal
and some effort to
reach it, no one
can live.

Fyodor Dostoyevsky

What do we live for, if it is not to make life less difficult for each other?

George Eliot

Life isn't about finding yourself. Life is about creating yourself.

George Bernard Shaw

If my doctor told me I had only six minutes to live, I wouldn't brood. I'd type a little faster.

Isaac Asimov

Perhaps our eyes need to be washed by our tears once in a while, so that we can see life with a clearer view again.

Alex Tan

Look at life through the windshield, not the rear-view mirror.

Byrd Baggett

Obstacles are those frightful
things you see when you
take your eyes off the goal.

Hannah More

The steeper the mountain,
the harder the climb, the
better the view from the
finishing line.

Anonymous

When you come to a
roadblock, take
a detour.

Mary Kay Ash

Everything is OK in
the end. If it's not OK,
then it's not the end.

Anonymous

Don't get your knickers in a
knot. Nothing is solved and
It Just makes you walk funny.

Kathryn Carpenter

Bad times have a scientific value. These are occasions a good learner would not miss.

Ralph Waldo Emerson

If you're already
walking on thin ice,
you might as
well dance.

Proverb

When asked if my cup is half-full or half-empty my only response is that I am thankful I have a cup.

Sam Lefkowitz

One doesn't discover new lands without consenting to lose sight of the shore for a very long time.

André Gide

My grandfather always said
that living is like licking
honey off a thorn.

Louis Adamic

The best way out is always through.

Robert Frost

I ask not for a lighter burden, but for broader shoulders.

Jewish proverb

It just wouldn't be a
picnic without
the ants.

Anonymous

When it is darkest,
men see the stars.

Ralph Waldo Emerson

Smooth seas do not make
skilful sailors.

African proverb

The darkest hour has only sixty minutes.

Morris Mandel

There's nothing that
cleanses your soul like
getting the hell kicked
out of you.

Woody Hayes

The average pencil is seven inches long, with just a half-inch eraser – in case you thought optimism was dead.

Robert Brault

I try to take one day at
a time, but sometimes
several days attack
me at once.

Jennifer Yane

The road to success is
dotted with many tempting
parking places.

Anonymous

If at first you don't
succeed, find out if the
loser gets anything.

Bill Lyon

When you come to the end
of your rope, tie a knot
and hang on.

Franklin D. Roosevelt

Even if you fall on your face, you're still moving forward.

Robert Gallagher

It's just life. Just live it.

Terri Guillemets

Ever tried. Ever failed. No matter. Try again. Fail again. Fail better.

Samuel Beckett, *Worstward Ho*

When life takes the wind out
of your sails, it is to test you
at the oars.

Robert Brault

Since the house is on fire let us warm ourselves.

Italian proverb

Water which is too
pure has no fish.

Ts'ai Ken T'an

Shoot for the moon. Even if
you miss, you'll land
among the stars.

Les Brown

I quit being afraid when my first venture failed and the sky didn't fall down.

Allen H. Neuharth

The season of failure
is the best time for
sowing the seeds
of success.

Paramahansa Yogananda

No one ever won a chess game by betting on each move. Sometimes you have to move backward to get a step forward.

Amar Gopal Bose

The trouble with
doing something right
the first time is that
nobody appreciates
how difficult it was.

Walt West

When we long for life
without difficulties,
remind us that
oaks grow strong in
contrary winds and
diamonds are made
under pressure.

Peter Marshall

It does no harm just once
in a while to acknowledge
that... there are people
in the country besides
politicians, entertainers
and criminals.

Charles Kuralt

The trouble with the
rat race is that even if
you win, you're
still a rat.

Lily Tomlin

Never be afraid to try; remember: amateurs built the ark, professionals built the *Titanic*.

Anonymous

The trouble with the future is that it usually arrives before we're ready for it.

Arnold H. Glasgow

Therefore, do not be anxious about tomorrow, for tomorrow will be anxious for itself. Let the day's own trouble be sufficient for the day.

Matthew 6:34

This life is not for complaint, but for satisfaction.

Henry David Thoreau

In school, you're taught
the lesson and then you're
given the test. In life, you're
glven a test that teaches
you a lesson.

Tom Bodett

A man's life is interesting
primarily when he has failed.

Georges Clemenceau

You can't turn back
the clock but you can
wind it up again.

Bonnie Prudden

When you arise in the morning, think of what a precious privilege it is to be alive – to breathe, to think, to enjoy and to love.

Marcus Aurelius Antoninus

Failures are like
skinned knees: painful
but superficial.

H. Ross Perot

Once the game is over, the
king and the pawn go back
into the same box.

Latin proverb

Birds sing after
a storm. Why
shouldn't we?

Rose Fitzgerald Kennedy

There has been much
tragedy in my life; at least
half of it actually happened.

Mark Twain

Love the moment.
Flowers grow out of
dark moments.

Corita Kent

Turn difficulties into learning opportunities.

Albert Einstein

Success and failure are
greatly overrated. But failure
gives you a whole lot more
to talk about.

Hildegard Knef

You can't have everything… where would you put it?

Steven Wright

Adversity has ever been
considered the state in
which a man most easily
becomes acquainted
with himself.

Samuel Johnson, 'The Rambler'

Rule number one is, don't sweat the small stuff. Rule number two is, it's all small stuff.

Robert Eliot

If you are irritated
by every rub, how
will your mirror be
polished?

Rumi, *Daylight*

If there must be trouble, let it be in my day, that my child may have peace.

Thomas Paine

When life looks like it's falling apart, it may just be falling in place.

Beverly Solomon

Life is a shipwreck,
but we must not forget
to sing in the lifeboats.

Voltaire

If you don't think every day is a good day, just try missing one.

Cavett Robert

The trouble with most
people is that they think
with their hopes or fears or
wishes rather than with
their minds.

Will Durant

I've decided that the stuff falling through the cracks is confetti and I'm having a party!

Betsy Cañas Garmon

Sometimes life's
hell. But hey!
Whatever gets the
marshmallows toasty.

J. Andrew Helt

There are two ways of meeting difficulties: you alter the difficulties or you alter yourself to meet them.

Phyllis Bottome

I can't complain, but
sometimes I still do.

Joe Walsh

A truly happy person is one who can enjoy the scenery while on a detour.

Anonymous

Always forgive your
enemies; nothing annoys
them so much.

Oscar Wilde

All things are difficult before they are easy.

Thomas Fuller

The necessity of the times,
more than ever, calls for
our utmost circumspection,
deliberation, fortitude,
and perseverance.

Samuel Adams

The greater the difficulty, the greater the glory.

Marcus Tullius Cicero

Difficulties strengthen the
mind, as labour does
the body.

Seneca

Perseverance, dear
my lord, keeps
honour bright.

William Shakespeare,
Troilus and Cressida

Our greatest glory is not in never falling, but in rising every time we fall.

Confucius

A problem is a chance
for you to do
your best.

Duke Ellington

Consider the postage stamp… it secures success through its ability to stick to one thing till it gets there.

Josh Billings

The elevator to success is out of order. You'll have to use the stairs... one step at a time.

Joe Girard

A dose of adversity is often
as needful as a dose
of medicine.

Proverb

The past is a
guidepost, not a
hitching post.

L. Thomas Holdcroft

A gem cannot be polished without friction, nor a man perfected without trials.

Chinese proverb

The difference between stumbling blocks and stepping stones is how you use them.

Anonymous

It is advisable that a person
know at least three things:
where they are, where
they are going, and what
they had best do under the
circumstances.

John Ruskin

The life of man
is a journey; a
journey that must be
travelled, however
bad the roads or the
accommodation.

Oliver Goldsmith

Courage is going from failure to failure without losing enthusiasm.

Winston Churchill

All of us could take a lesson
from the weather; it pays no
attention to criticism.

Anonymous

You miss one hundred per cent of the shots you don't take.

Wayne Gretzky

Nobody says you must laugh, but a sense of humour can help you overlook the unattractive, tolerate the unpleasant... and smile through the day.

Ann Landers

Scar tissue is stronger
than regular tissue.
Realise the strength,
move on.

Henry Rollins

Life appears to me too short to be spent in nursing animosity, or registering wrongs.

Charlotte Brontë, *Jane Eyre*

If your ship doesn't
come in, swim
out to it.

Jonathan Winters

I have a simple philosophy:
fill what's empty; empty
what's full; scratch where
it itches.

Alice Roosevelt Longworth

Your life is an
occasion. Rise to it.

Suzanne Weyn

The harder you fall, the higher you bounce.

Doug Horton

Life is 'trying things to
see if they work'.

Ray Bradbury

After a year in therapy, my
psychiatrist said to me,
'Maybe life isn't
for everyone.'

Larry Brown

Make the most of your regrets… To regret deeply is to live afresh.

Henry David Thoreau

I've learned that when
you harbour bitterness,
happiness will dock
elsewhere.

Andy Rooney

It has been my philosophy of life that difficulties vanish when faced boldly.

Isaac Asimov

I take a simple view
of life: keep your eyes
open and get on
with it.

Laurence Olivier

Think of all the beauty
still left around you
and be happy.

Anne Frank

Failure is only the
opportunity to begin again,
only this time more wisely.

Henry Ford

Turn your face to the
sun and the shadows
fall behind you.

Maori proverb

One of the best lessons you
can learn in life is to master
how to remain calm.

Catherine Pulsifer

You can't make an
omelette without
breaking eggs.

Proverb

Be comfortable being
uncomfortable. It may get
tough, but it's a small price
to pay for living a dream.

Peter McWilliams

Never, never, never give up.

Winston Churchill

Experience: that most brutal
of teachers.

C. S. Lewis

The score never
interested me, only
the game.

Mae West

Things turn out best for the people who make the best of the way things turn out.

John Wooden

Tough times never last.
Tough people do.

Robert Schuller

Shit happens.

American proverb

KEEP
CALM

AND

DRINK
UP

KEEP CALM AND DRINK UP

£4.99

ISBN: 978 1 84953 102 3

'*In victory, you deserve champagne;
in defeat, you need it.*'

Napoleon Bonaparte

BAD ADVICE FOR GOOD PEOPLE.

Keep Calm and Carry On, a World War Two government poster, struck a chord in recent difficult times when a stiff upper lip and optimistic energy were needed again. But in the long run it's a stiff drink and flowing spirits that keep us all going.

Here's a book packed with proverbs and quotations showing the wisdom to be found at the bottom of the glass.

NOW
PANIC

AND

FREAK
OUT